American Indians Dream

A Movement of Our Own

STEVE RUSSELL

ISBN: 1499225881
ISBN-13 9781499225884

CONTENTS

Our nation was born in genocide when it embraced the doctrine that the original American, the Indian, was an inferior race. Even before there were large numbers of Negroes on our shore, the scar of racial hatred had already disfigured colonial society. From the sixteenth century forward, blood flowed in battles over racial supremacy. We are perhaps the only nation which tried as a matter of national policy to wipe out its indigenous population. Moreover, we elevated that tragic experience into a noble crusade. Indeed, even today we have not permitted ourselves to reject or feel remorse for this shameful episode. Our literature, our films, our drama, our folklore all exalt it.

Dr. Martin Luther King, Jr.

1 THE DISENROLLMENT EPIDEMIC

Professor David Wilkins, a learned and decent man whose work I greatly admire, published an op-ed at Indian Country Today Media Network expressing his dismay at language chosen by the Chief Judge of the Nooksack Tribal Court in a disenrollment decision: "Why a Native judge would consider tribal nationhood inferior to US statehood is a frightening perception to fathom."

The judge, upholding the disenrollment, had presumed to console the people stripped of their citizenship by expressing that it was not as if they have become stateless persons or lost as much as they would have lost with U.S. citizenship. Professor Wilkins' dismay was directed not at the holding of the case, which supported the sovereign authority of the Nooksack Nation to be stupid, but to the Chief Judge's assertion that tribal enrollment is of less legal import than loss of US citizenship.

Nowhere in Professor Wilkins's critique of the opinion does he touch the essential argument the judge made: "While the impact on the disenrollee is serious and detrimental, it is not akin to becoming stateless."

I propose a thought experiment. Suppose that the persons subject to disenrollment by the Nooksacks had US citizenship not by the right of birth set out in the Fourteenth Amendment, but rather a derivative citizenship based on the Indian Citizenship Act of 1924.

Suppose that upon disenrollment, US passports had to be surrendered, Social Security numbers cancelled. Would that not be at least a different kettle of fish, if not two seasons of *The Deadliest Catch*?

Disenrollees would be insulted and diminished. They may have lost affirmative action consideration if it existed anymore. They would have lost any benefits that flow though membership in the Nooksack Social Club—for so it will render itself by its own actions.

Disenrollees are not stateless persons in two

senses. The first is that they still have passports and the consular rights those passports confer. They still have Social Security cards and access to the anemic social safety net those cards confer.

The second is that they are still citizens of the Nooksack Nation to the degree it still exists, as the Cherokee Nation does, as the Six Nations do, as the Navajo Nation does…I am not fully informed how many tribal nations survive, but I'm certain that it's a substantially smaller number than can be found in 25 *Code of Federal Regulations* Part 83.

You don't get your tribal citizenship from the U.S. government.

Either something of your tribal identity, your peoplehood, survives as more than family folklore or it does not.

If it does, it's an important political question to what degree your tribal citizenship conflicts with your U.S. or Canadian or Mexican citizenship?

What would you say to Charles Curtis, a Kaw who served as Vice President of the United States? As far as that goes, what do you say to me when I sit as a Texas state judge under both the Stars and Stripes and the Lone Star?

If this is too esoteric, I'll notice that the oath of office I took did not differ substantially from the oath I took upon enlistment in the U.S. armed forces. In my day, more Indian young men took that oath than did not. Did we swear falsely?

Historians tell us that the modern nation-state was born in 1648, when power passed on paper from Divine Authority to various European warlords in the Peace of Westphalia. That's a "truth" on the same level as democracy being born in 1215 (Magna Carta) or the Common Law beginning in 1066, when a thug called William the Bastard changed his historical identity to William the Conqueror at the Battle of Hastings. No ordinary person in 1066 or 1215 or 1648 would have noticed much of anything, except for men under arms and the warlords who commanded them.

Right now, we live in a time when the nation-state is becoming less relevant to human organization. Labor and capital ignore national borders. Within nations, "sovereign" authority is split among localities because it's more efficient and because democracy is now the ascendant ideology and people demand local control of local issues. National governments simply direct traffic.

The time when sovereignty meant fealty to an individual, the sovereign, is long gone. This is the age of bureaucracy and nation-states do not control all the bureaus.

So, did I swear falsely when I joined the military?

No, for two reasons. One is that a threat to the U.S. is a threat to the Cherokee Nation and the other is that the Cherokee Nation does not field an army.

What about when I became a judge? What if the Cherokee Nation sued the state of Texas? I sat in lawsuits all the time where the state of Texas was a party, because my court was in the capital. A federal judge from Oklahoma is not disqualified in a case between Oklahoma and the United States. So why would I be unable to hear a lawsuit involving my tribal nation, any more than my state, county, city, school board, or any of the myriad taxing districts Texas has created to maintain the myth that Texans are not taxed?

Assuming that a federally recognized tribal government is the same as the traditional government of the tribal nation (a big assumption), the status of that government is a question of what the U.S. calls "federalism"---what questions are apportioned to what level of authority? Who holds the power to decide?

What happens if the interests of the *real* tribal government conflict with the interests of the U.S. government and the dispute cannot be resolved by negotiation or litigation?

I do not think going to war is a live option, but placing ourselves outside of U.S. law and/or state law certainly is. This is what we call in the social change trade "direct action." Mohandas Gandhi did it in South Africa and India. Nelson Mandela did it in South Africa. Martin Luther King and César Chávez did it in the U.S. An issue that cannot be reached by direct action is an issue without much consequence to ordinary people.

There comes a time, if your fundamental interests are ignored, when a demand not worth killing for is at least worth dying for or, more likely, going to jail for.

I've had many, many conversations with Indians of many tribes about what they think of their federally recognized tribal governments. Very few trust tribal governments any more than they trust the feds, and nobody trusts the feds. To my knowledge, no tribal government has undertaken the training of tribal citizens in the discipline required to take direct action, to go to war with the United States.

If that's the case, it seems to me that we will do what we are told if US interests conflict with tribal interests, and all a disenrollee has lost is a ride on whatever gravy train the tribal social club is conducting. The greedy clowns cannot take your tribal citizenship away because they didn't give it to you.

You were born with it, and the significance of it

is whatever you can make by courage and perseverance. Wow, that sounds brutal. It does. It puts us in exactly the same position our ancestors were in. I get my Cherokee citizenship from Dragging Canoe and John Ross and many others, because they had courage and perseverance. Everybody has a tribal history of heroic resistance to colonization if his or her tribal nation still exists today.

To the extent disenrollments are not driven by simple greed to cut a pie into fewer slices or, like the disenrollment of the Cherokee freedmen, a factional electoral advantage, tribal governments have an issue identical to that of conventional nation-states. Political geographer Marco Antonsich calls it "the crisis of the hyphen," and it comes from the globalization of labor. The US has Mexican-Americans; the Europeans have Turkish-Germans and Algerian-French. Many of the hyphenated citizen situations are exacerbated by special immigration privileges between colonies and mother countries.

We have white Indians and black Indians, but color is a more fraught classification than the hyphen, because it feeds the myth of "race."

Nation-states have made two classes of response to the crisis of the hyphen. The first is to rewrite national identity in purely political terms. This solution has been foisted upon U.S. tribal nations by the line of Supreme Court authority that exempts Indians from aspects of equal protection law driven by the Fourteenth Amendment. Congress can, according to this line of authority, treat Indians differently from others without a "compelling governmental interest" to which the difference is "narrowly tailored" because the distinction is political rather than racial.

The second response to the rise of hyphenated citizens runs in the opposite direction. Some nation-states have tightened their immigration laws to demand tests of cultural competence or at least cultural compatibility. I have argued that, for instance, if the Cherokee Nation does not takes steps along these lines, Cherokee identity will be reduced to an accident of bureaucracy that will get no respect from the public, something that will eventually take away the respect in law. As all Indian tribes register exogamous marriages and blood quantum requirements work their magic, the Cherokee Nation is surfing a demographic wave that will get everybody wet eventually.

A tribal democracy is unlikely to stand for arranged marriages or for exclusion of grandchildren, and the latter is a ticket to extinction.

There is a sense in which this political problem is going to solve itself. Our standing in U.S. law is being swiftly eroded, and the protections offered in international law are not robust.

The "real" tribal identity, peoplehood, carries with it a sense of solidarity and purpose that will enable defense by direct action, outside of law, and as long as the demands are reasonable public opinion in the US will support the Indian side. If tribal governments remain mired in corruption and self-seeking, we will lack the cohesion required for militant defense and we will end up doing as we are told.

We are not worthy of what our ancestors struggled to defend if the BIA denies our existence *and we agree with them*. As to the federally recognized tribal governments, if they have lost the ability to find their hind legs, then they can be opposed by direct action as well. The cohesion and purpose that direct action requires is perhaps the most important tribal heritage. Use it or lose it, but don't whine.

2 FREE AND INDEPENDENT?

Because traditional Cherokee people taught me a profound insight that I've claimed for my own, "the spirit world takes care of its own business," I understand arguments about religion to be for amusement only. I still like to win, and any advocate knows that anger is the enemy of clear thought.

So I come out of the chute describing what theologians call "the Abrahamic faiths" (Judaism, Christianity, Islam) as "monotheistic, patriarchal desert cults." This serves nicely to place the burden of proof where it belongs, on anybody who maintains that the rich mythos of Mesopotamia and Northern Africa has anything to do with peoples who already own their rich indigenous mythos.

When they finish sputtering, my first question is "Which part of my definition do you dispute?"

So it is in the realm of politics with "domestic,

dependent nations," but we are the ones sputtering.

I have written both in my first book, *Sequoyah Rising* (Carolina Academic Press 2010) and in the pages of *Indian Country Today* about the extra-constitutional nature of this supposedly constitutional definition of the status of American Indians in U.S. law. It's not in the Constitution. Chief Justice John Marshall made it up.

John Marshall was nobody's fool, so which part of his definition do we dispute? In the beginning, all three parts.

The original thirteen colonies each made land claims that could only be described as fantastical, and none today exists in their originally imagined borders. The occupants to the west were Indians, and who was "domestic" compared to whom was a fair argument.

At the edges of colonial settlements, we were interdependent. Indians never took up gunsmithing or large scale smelting or making textiles by machine, but we considered firearms and metal and cloth as necessary then as we consider the Internet now. We usually had plenty to trade with the colonists.

"Nations" were units of social organization that most historians date from the Peace of Westphalia in 1648, which ratified the division of the Holy Roman Empire among European warlords. The colonization of the Americas was already under way in 1648, but by the time Marshall wrote about us 150 years later, nations were as dominant as transnational corporations are today.

From Marshall's point of view, we needed to be domestic so we could not pursue an independent foreign policy, playing the U.S., Canada, England, Spain, France, and Russia against each other. We did it anyway, of course.

We had to be nations to sign the treaties that provided the legal fig leaves for acquisition of our property.

Dependent was the keystone concept that enforced all the rest, and so it remains. We were made dependent on purpose. It makes me grind my teeth when I hear our political enemies hold forth about the squalor on some reservations or the casino riches on others. Who forced us to live in squalor? Who gambles in Indian casinos?

In modern times, North America is the story of two behemoths, the United States and Canada. Mexico gets considered part of Latin America, a triumph of culture over geography that, if carried to its logical conclusion, would split off much of the southwestern U.S. Indian nations are physically located within these behemoths, making us "domestic" from the point of view of colonists who no longer remember colonization.

"Nations" are a kind of cosmic joke of the 21st century, as transnational corporations have slipped their national moorings to thumb their noses at political control. The U.S., which recognizes "sovereignty" in the several states, is in a particularly strange place, with the principles of "federalism" splitting authority between state and federal governments. These principles provide a ready mooring for a robust understanding of Indian sovereignty if we could ever break loose from the web woven by John Marshall.

The spider in that web remains "dependent." No entity can ever assert sovereignty from a condition of dependence. Anybody who has raised a teenager knows the feelings that arise in the people who pay the bills when told they don't get to call the shots.

My Indian Country Today Media Network colleagues are fond of "free and independent" as a description of the once and future status of Indian nations. Indian individuals were certainly freer than the colonists, and our governments were also more independent until taught to want things they could not produce.

In modern times, Indians living under Indian governments are wont to compare their degree of "freedom" to colonial aspirations set out in the Bill of Rights and find freedom elusive. "Independent" has little meaning for nation-states in the age of globalization. *A fortiori*, there's little independent about the state of Texas in Gov. Rick Perry's secessionist fantasies or the recent referendum in Colorado over seceding not from the U.S., but from Colorado. Do they really intend to give up the Broncos?

Seriously, our political future is at a functional fork in the road, and neither fork leads to a restoration of mythical American Indian kings who could sit beside European kings as political power personified, sovereigns.

In one direction, we have a legal status roughly comparable to labor unions, less powerful than corporations in that "members"—not "citizens"---have legal rights enforceable against tribal government and guaranteed by the colonial powers.

In the other direction, we have a governmental role in a federal system that we define for ourselves by direct action because John Marshall's made up structure no longer fits the realities on the ground. The first step to shaping our own realities on the ground is putting an end to imposed dependence. Some tribal governments are better fixed than others to accomplish as much self-sufficiency as states, but those that fail are destined for the path of glorified social clubs.

As long as we remain dependent in fact, discussions of sovereignty are for amusement only.

3 LET IT BLEED?

Ideas, like people, can bleed. Unlike people, ideas do not die easily, even the worst of ideas. If you have lost a loved one, you know that palpable sense of wishing them back, undoing their fate so as to undo your own. So it is with bad ideas, but in the world of ideas the wish can easily be the father to the thought, and the thought to the action.

I look at a map showing what members of Congress think it was wise to shut down the government to gain leverage in unrelated matters and I see a map of the Confederate States of America. The Civil War was fought over slavery, lost, and recast in the history books as a war over "state's rights."

The legacy of slavery was the Black Codes and Jim Crow. The legacy of "state's rights" is the "right" to living conditions unbefitting a modern industrialized nation. The U.S. accepts these living conditions on Indian reservations unless tribal governments can parlay what they have into something better, but the U.S. also accepts the same in entire states.

Only one of the Confederate states, Arkansas, accepted the expansion of Medicaid in Obamacare. The body count among poor people from the failure to expand Medicaid will be substantial, but I'm not convinced it will move the voters of those states. The statistics on education in the Confederacy back in the fifties were horrifying, and they led to President John Kennedy pressing to do something about it on the federal level, because the states simply would not.

The Confederacy used to be governed by Dixiecrats because the party of Lincoln was the enemy during the Civil War and Reconstruction. Dixiecrats became modern Republicans, who have thrown Lincoln under the bus, along with Theodore Roosevelt, the progressive Republican who bequeathed the national park system and anti-trust law to a GOP now hostile to both.

The historical Confederacy is such a wonderful place to live according to the numbers.

Lower taxes. No unions. More guns. More Jesus. Lower literacy rates. Higher mortality and morbidity rates. Lower per capita income. More homicides, illegal and legal. Does this resemble any reservations you know, excepting the part about legal homicides, tribal governments being limited in modern times to opting into the federal death penalty rather than imposing their own?

And now, the U.S. has governmental paralysis by a suicidal minority based in the South, so save your Confederate money to buy some dead political science texts.

Turn to World War II in the history of ideas and we can say that the Nazis lost everything, correct? Not exactly. They lost Hitler and his immediate henchmen.

Nazis fled to South Africa and formed the Nationalist Party, leading a white minority to oppress a black majority until very recently.

Nazis fled to Latin America, and our neighbors to the south have only recently emerged from a game of musical chairs played by right wing dictators (often of Germanic surname) to music supplied by the Central Intelligence Agency during the Cold War.

Those are real exertions of power. Reasonable persons can differ about how concerned we should be over the neo-Nazi parties worshipping the memory of Hitler everywhere from Germany to all of the victorious allied nations.

While it's true that you can't kill a good idea permanently, it's fair to wonder when bad ideas meet their natural demise?

Consider the Ghost Dance, and the thoughts to which it can claim paternity.

The American bison absolutely can return to the Plains, but it will take careful stewardship over generations. The largest herd living today is run by a rich white guy, but several tribes are involved in the effort and the bison was hunted close enough to extinction that we can't be picky how the genes are preserved.

The colonists absolutely cannot be pushed back into the ocean. They have nowhere to go.

I presume there's no need to discuss bulletproof regalia, since Quanah Parker had exactly the same collision with modernity at Adobe Walls?

Federal Indian control law is a house of cards, built with one bad idea balanced upon another. It could collapse if a solid majority of the U.S. Supreme Court ever heaved a frustrated sigh and gave it up as impossible to fix.

Then what?

Do Indian nations become social clubs revolving around historical grievances and genealogy?

Do Indian nations assert their free and

independent status in the quickly becoming obsolete form of the nation-state with a modern Ghost Dance where the opposing weapon will no longer be bullets but more likely bemused tolerance?

Or do we plunge into a political war to define the role of tribal governments within a federal system that was left undefined in the Constitution because we were outside both the process and the authority? Understanding that the outcome will be hotly contested and therefore uncertain? And understanding that lots of people might get put in jail before it's over?

American Indian political science, the art and praxis of governing ourselves, has been stunted by decades of dependence. The good ideas are bleeding along with the bad ideas. It's up to us which ones survive.

4 *LE NOIR ET LE ROUGE*

Anniversaries matter in the short run as memory markers and in the long run they become traditions. The year 1963 was the 100th anniversary of the signing of the Emancipation Proclamation, and it was used by activists of the time to take another step toward emancipation on the economic front. On August 28, 2013, we noted—those of us who cared to note—the 50th anniversary of the March on Washington for Jobs and Freedom.

American Indians have a complicated relationship with African-Americans in general and their freedom struggle in particular. We have in common that we inhabit a nation founded on theft of Indian land and black labor at a time when land and labor were the primary sources of wealth. Those twin thefts have created a paradise for the descendants of the thieves and a multi-generational crapshoot for the descendants of the victims.

For some individual blacks and Indians who were born with or acquired the grit and luck it takes to play a stacked deck against the house, America has fulfilled the great land of opportunity mythos that, ironically, still works better for immigrants than for those of us born here.

Historically, laws that denied education and the right to vote and to testify in court often applied to blacks and Indians alike. Laws against interracial marriage put us in the same category as well.

White people told blacks that Indians were dangerous savages, and so sent the "buffalo soldiers" to fight the Comanche-Kiowa Alliance for white dominance on the Southern Plains.

White people told Indians that blacks were sub-humans, and too many "civilized" Indians, my own people included, took up the ignominious historical role of slaveholders.

While blacks and Indians were marked for similar roles as victims, blacks had certain disadvantages that did not burden Indians. African-Americans are tribal peoples completely ripped from their roots. If they escaped, they had nowhere to go, no allies. Being darker than Indians, those who were able to intermarry carried their inferiority of color for more generations.

Slave rebellions were few and short-lived. Gabriel Prosser in 1800; Denmark Vesey in 1822; Nat Turner in 1831. American Indians, with superior knowledge of the land and numerous allies, fought the colonists to a standstill for as long as they could play off various colonial powers against each other. After the Civil War, when the U.S. could finally focus all military might on the rebellious tribes of the Great Plains, the shooting pretty well ended in 25 years.

By the time it ended, Indians had given a good account of themselves in too many military campaigns to count. The shooting wars ended with the defeat of the alliance of the Great Sioux Nation and the Cheyenne and Arapaho on the Northern Plains and the Kiowa and Comanche on the Southern Plains, but many peoples fought bravely for generations. For this resistance, we honor names like Tecumseh, Pontiac, Rolling Thunder, Dragging Canoe, Cochise, and Osceola.

One of Osceola's generals who fits in this discussion was the redoubtable John Horse, a man of Seminole and African descent. The Seminoles, some of whom never did surrender to the white invaders in Florida, often gave African slaves somewhere to go if they wanted to put up a fight for freedom.

After the end of the Civil War enabled the defeat of the Plains Indians, the promise of freedom for African slaves died with Abraham Lincoln and with the neutering of the 14th Amendment by the US Supreme Court. The Jim Crow laws put African-Americans back under the economic thumb of white settlers as sharecroppers on the lands where they used to be slaves.

The promise of an Indian Territory for the "civilized" Indians died with Oklahoma statehood in 1907. Henry Dawes had passed the General Allotment Act in 1887 to destroy common landholding among Indians and enable vast tracts of formerly reservation land to be declared "surplus." Indians would honor their history by never forgetting the leaders of the litigation and disobedience campaigns against the Dawes Act: the Kiowa Lone Wolf, the Creek Chitto Harjo, and the Cherokee Redbird Smith.

The Dawes Act destroyed tribal economies and put Indians who had previously been prosperous back under the economic thumb of white settlers.

This economic raw deal for blacks and Indians continued to be enabled by color prejudice. Indians could often "pass" after three generations of exogamy; blacks remained subject to the "one drop rule."

It was economically convenient for the settlers that one drop of black blood rendered a person black and fit only for manual labor. It was similarly convenient that any intermarriage by Indians rendered the offspring white, and therefore ineligible for what compensation was offered when Indians were separated from their property. Because of tribal traditions, this never blossomed into a "reverse one drop rule," but the federal government did what it could by using Indian blood quantum to determine which tribal citizens would "qualify" to sell their allotments.

This was American prosperity. Labor stolen from Africans bringing wealth from land stolen from Indians, peoples who were taught to hate each other by their exploiters and kept at the bottom of the education and economic ladders with the easy metric of color prejudice, and kept from doing anything about it at the ballot box with laws that declared them unfit to vote.

World War II, 1939-1945, was a global horror. It caused the deaths of millions of innocent people and brought forth what we now call "weapons of mass destruction." The one good thing to be said for it is the fight was too big for white people to do it alone, and after risking their lives to make other peoples free, nonwhite American GIs came home determined to do the same for their relatives. It was this new determination that led directly to the events of August 28, 1963.

5 DREAMS DEFERRED

After World War II, a new phase of resistance came forward, and when the struggle became nonviolent, Indians lost their claim to greatest effectiveness. Even though violence as a political tactic had long faded, WWII seemed to make all exploited nonwhites more "uppity."

Historically black colleges filled up in no time, and blacks demanded entry to other state institutions to use their GI Bill entitlements. Denied, they filed lawsuits that forced integration of graduate schools, undergraduate schools, and finally K-12.

Indian GIs returning from the war headed up the litigation that opened up the right to vote for Indians living on the reservations in New Mexico and Arizona and they, too, moved to use their GI Bill rights.

Hispanic veterans in 1948 organized the

American GI Forum, under the motto "Education Is Our Freedom and Freedom Should Be Everybody's Business." This was a time when Mexican-Americans were still segregated and denied the equal treatment promised by the Treaty of Guadalupe-Hidalgo in the southwestern U.S., and most of the white people doing the segregating could not tell Hispanics from Indians.

Asians, too, had been subject to race-based discrimination, and it was the GI Bill that bought education for one of the best friends American Indians ever had in Congress, Sen. Daniel Inouye, Medal of Honor veteran of the storied 442nd Regimental Combat Team, the most decorated infantry regiment in the history of the US Army.

Everybody was moving, although, ironically, the oppressed minorities by and large moved separately on what became a common freedom agenda:

*Equal access to education

*Equal access to the ballot box

*Equal access to public accommodations

*Jobs, jobs, jobs, and at a decent wage

Indians were on board with this agenda and, to the extent the mainstream civil rights movement succeeded, Indians benefitted when they lived in the dominant culture or were forced to visit reservation border towns.

They had, however, a different set of demands of the U.S. government, demands for segregation rather than integration—self-government on their own lands. They also had a different basis for those demands, in some cases treaties and in other cases respect for cultures that far antedated the US Constitution, to which Indians were not parties.

Other minorities, with exceptions like Sen. Inouye and African-American activist and comedian Dick Gregory, did not understand Indian demands. Some Indians even came to resent the successes of the mainstream civil rights movement, in spite of insightful explanations of the differing goals by Vine Deloria, Jr. and others. Even within the African-American movement, all was not sweetness and light.

At the March on Washington, the distinguished literary lion James Baldwin was not allowed to speak, as he was expected to be too inflammatory. The youngest speaker, original Freedom Rider (now Congressman) John Lewis, had his speech toned down substantially by the leadership by cutting, among other lines, "...we will march though the South, through the heart of Dixie, the way Sherman did. We shall pursue our own scorched earth policy and burn Jim Crow to the ground---nonviolently." Malcolm X called the demonstration "a circus" and objected to allowing whites to participate.

The role of women was limited to entertaining. Marian Anderson, Mary Travers, Odetta and Joan Baez sang in front of the largest civil rights demonstration in history, and it was the great gospel singer, Mahalia Jackson, who contributed to the pivotal moment we remember, when we choose to remember, that day. Her majestic voice rings out, as Dr. Martin Luther King, Jr. pauses, "Tell them about the dream, Martin!"

At that point, the Baptist preacher departs from the prepared remarks of his call-and-response sermon and improvises on lines he had used many times before. Those lines now, in the history books, title the speech: "I have a dream."

We are peoples of oral tradition. We understand and honor great oratory.

The FBI also understood great oratory. Two days after the speech, the head of COINTELPRO (COunter INTELligence PROgram), William Sullivan, wrote for the record of King's "powerful demagogic speech," and that program was turned against the Southern Christian Leadership Conference and also against King as an individual. The American Indian Movement would later join the SCLC as a target of COINTELPRO when several charismatic leaders attracted national attention.

The man said he had a dream. He didn't say it would be easy, and he knew it could cost him his life, which it did. Fifty years off from the Great March on Washington, the struggle is far from over, and nobody is farther behind on the freedom agenda than American Indians.

The 2012 election was held in the face of state government voter suppression laws aimed at Indians, blacks, and Hispanics not seen since the Voting Rights Act of 1965, and the Supreme Court has since pulled the teeth of that law, as well as the Indian Child Welfare Act, two civil rights laws that have been perhaps too successful for the comfort of some.

Voting rights remain necessary to addressing the rest of the agenda, education and jobs and, in the case of Indians, tribal sovereignty. On July 30, 2013, there was a meeting at the White House to address the attacks on voting rights, and it's interesting to note who attended besides elected officials:

*Barbara Arnwine, President & Executive Director, the Lawyers' Committee for Civil Rights Under Law

*Roslyn Brock, Chairman, National Association for the Advancement of Colored People Board of Directors

*John Echohawk, Executive Director, Native American Rights Fund

*Margaret Fung, Executive Director, Asian American Legal Defense and Education Fund

*Wade Henderson, President and CEO, The Leadership Conference on Civil and Human Rights

*Sherrilyn Ifill, President and Director-Counsel, NAACP Legal Defense and Educational Fund, Inc.

*Marc Morial, President and CEO, National Urban League

*Mee Moua, President and Executive Director, Asian Americans Advancing Justice

*Janet Murguia, President & CEO, National Council of La Raza

*Laura Murphy, Director, American Civil Liberties Union

*Thomas Saenz, President & General Counsel, The Mexican American Legal Defense and Educational Fund
*Al Sharpton, President & Founder, National Action Network

It's a measure of the change since 1963 that this meeting happened at the White House.

It's a measure of the lack of change since 1963 that this meeting was necessary.

I hope it's a measure of what we've learned in the past 50 years that, at least on the voting rights issue, we stand together. I hope we understand now that if white people who believe in the promise of freedom stand together with African-Americans, Indians, Asian Americans and Hispanic Americans, then we are no longer a minority.

Leaving aside the new and fantastical way Indians are counted for the Census, we remain less than one percent of the population of a land where we used to be one hundred percent. Therefore, we must do politics with allies or we will not be heard.

We, too, have a dream.

6 MLK'S LEGACY

Martin Luther King, Jr. famously told the nation, "I have a dream." Less famously, he said on April 3, 1968: "Like anybody, I would like to live a long life. Longevity has its place. But I'm not concerned about that now. I just want to do God's will. And He's allowed me to go up to the mountain. And I've looked over. And I've seen the Promised Land. I may not get there with you. But I want you to know tonight, that we, as a people, will get to the Promised Land!"

The next day, April 4, he was taken by an assassin's bullet.

I asserted of MLK's most famous speech that Indians, too, have a dream. A fine rhetorical flourish, if I do say so, but is it true? And if it is true, does our devotion to that dream match MLK's?

Or do we have 566 dreams that conflict, each

with the other? If that's so, there is nothing traditional about those dreams, since many of the 566 federally recognized tribes are peoples separated by accident of history. Look no farther than my people, split into three governments with three sets of enrollment criteria and only one with a serious land base.

I must ask whether the conflicts we have among us rise to the importance of MLK's dream? I look around Indian country and I see conflicts not over fundamental values but over jurisdiction and over market share.

I see companies get contracts for tribal casino business using opaque practices that allow all tribes to get screwed by telling tribe A they get a better deal than the other tribes and so it must be kept secret...and, of course, telling tribes B, C, and D the same thing.

I see tribes taking sides in the bureaucratic process of federal recognition on the theory that pie is being divided up and their slice will diminish if more tribal governments are on the dole or more casinos are enabled.

I see companies feeding at the tribal trough because, we are told, our people are ignorant of the necessary skills. If that's true, why do we not require those companies that profit from our ignorance to remove that ignorance as a cost of doing business on Indian land?

I see tribal governments justifying their existence by reference to tradition and hiding their misdeeds behind tribal sovereignty, while they provide nothing for the most traditional people among us and fail to assert sovereignty for any purpose but short-term gain.

Ask an Indian activist about tribal sovereignty and the activist will favor it as an article of faith. Ask an Indian activist about their own tribal government and they will claim it has the morals of pond scum and the attention span of a fruit fly.

Governments are governments and always shall be governments. They do as they are told when the people are organized to tell them and when the people are not organized they do as they please, building tiny empires for outsized egos and sucking sustenance from our collective body like so many remora fish.

To put it another way, we get the government we deserve, our dessert being measured by the amount of attention we are willing to pay and the amount of risk we are willing to take.

When African-Americans finally had enough, they determined to risk their lives in pursuit of a dream deferred since the end of the Civil War.

So I ask again, do American Indians have a dream? If so, how much blood is it worth? Not anybody else's blood, but our own.

If we have no dream, or the dream is not worth risk, we should, as the kids say online, STFU.

We claim tradition as our pole star, and if this were true, it would be a problem. It's not true. The traditions about which we are most vociferous come from the horse cultures and the horse cultures did not exist on this continent until the Spanish colonists proved unable to keep track of their livestock.

The peyote culture goes back at least 10,000 years, but where would it be without Quanah Parker?

The pueblos have some of the strongest claims to tradition among us, but even they would have a hard time without not only the things but also the ideas modernism has wrought.

I keep coming back to Vine Deloria, Jr.'s observation that white people vote for morons and Indians vote for crooks. It provokes an involuntary smile even as it stings, like much of Deloria's thought.

If he's right, why is he right?

It seems to me that our crooks are some of the smartest political scientists we've produced. They look at the structure. The money comes in from the feds or from the casino or from the extractive industry and it is the source of continuing power. As long as this engine turns, I and mine can take a reasonable cut and I shall be important to outsiders.

One reason you will never see me run to represent outlanders on the Cherokee Tribal Council is that I have no problem with people who stay in the homelands and keep the culture having more rights that those of us who left to chase things the homelands can't offer. But another serious reason is that I look at outlander Cherokees as a nascent tax base.

Indians paying taxes? To tribal government?

My illusions, if such they are, come from having worked for César Chávez. He had the poorest workers in the country, migrant farm workers, paying union dues before the union had a contract or any prospect of a contract. His organizers made the same as Chávez made, room and board and five bucks a week for spending money, which would be about forty bucks in today's dollars.

But Chávez was an honest man, and my tribal government is a den of thieves!

For whom do they work, this den of thieves? If you don't pay taxes, you are not paying them. They owe more of their keep to the feds than they owe to you. Why should they answer to you and why should you bother to make them? You have no skin in the game other than a place at the trough.

And there's another political science catch that most Indians understand in their viscera: sovereignty and dependence cannot coexist. Your tribal government can assert itself against the federal government only to the extent that it could survive without the federal government. The list of tribes that could do that is short.

In my first book, *Sequoyah Rising,* I set out many ways that tribal governments are failing to use the powers that they have under current law as the U.S. Supreme Court bleeds those powers away and the white peoples' rights movement outflanks us.

What I failed to fully appreciate is that tribal governments, as presently constituted, are more of the problem than they are of the solution. That is not, however, the fault of the people who serve in them.

We, the people of the tribal nations, have allowed ourselves to be yoked up to non-traditional processes that respond to a system of perverse incentives. Unless we, as indigenous political scientists, can find ways to align tribal government incentives to our interests, we will continue to elect crooks, since kleptocracy is the only option on the table.

This is not an argument against voting. Rather, it is recognition that voting is necessary but not sufficient. Government—national, state, tribal, city---is a means to an end, the dream MLK found worth his life. For us, no less than for African-Americans, the dream is to make the decisions that affect our lives. MLK, in a 1957 speech, said that without the right to vote, "I cannot make up my own mind — it is made up for me. I cannot live as a democratic citizen, observing the laws I have helped enact — I can only submit to the edict of others."

If we are satisfied with the edict of others, if we have no dream to call our own, then discontent is merely our signature political sport as fry bread is our signature food, and one is about as nourishing as the other.

7 DREAMING IN SPADES AND HEARTS

In this series of essays keying on Martin Luther King's iconic *I Have a Dream* speech," I've asked Indians to dream. I've asked whether we have dreams worth risk and multi-generational effort. Without dreams, it's hard to see how we have an Indian Martin Luther King or an Indian César Chávez. It's hard to see a need for the tactics set out by the other kind of Indian, Mohandas Karamchand Gandhi, an English-educated Hindu lawyer whose life ended as MLK's, by an assassin's hand. By the time of his death, Gandhi carried the honorific "Mahatma." In English, "Great Soul."

I am not a Hindu like Gandhi or a Catholic like Chávez or even a Baptist like King, though my great grandfather was a full blood Cherokee Baptist preacher. I am a mere student of political science and history who can see what works. Gandhian tactics are only available to those willing to risk their freedom and perhaps their lives.

While Indians have few relevant traditions—we did do some non-cooperation—Gandhi suggests that the highest level of organizing is "parallel government." We already have parallel governments.

Those governments do not, as a rule, dream intergenerational dreams or offer much to those who do. Therefore, should dreamers run for tribal office?

I cannot speak for others. You don't tell others how to order their lives. It's enough that you order your own in a constructive way. For me to run for tribal office would waste other people's money, since I have none of my own to waste.

I am not a Christian. That disqualifies me. Oklahoma is the buckle on the Bible Belt, and that's a major reason I left.

I favor marriage equality in tribal law. It's one of those rare issues where what is traditional and what is future-oriented are one in the same. That disqualifies me.

I don't support the grief the Cherokee Nation has given the United Keetoowah Band. Fighting among ourselves is idiocy. Here I lose the votes of those who value market share.

I do support the historical and legal claim for citizenship of the former Cherokee slaves. Indian tribes who abrogate treaties are playing with dynamite and giving up moral high ground that is our major asset. Here I lose the racist vote.

I do not have any problem with people living within the Nation having greater rights than outlanders, provided the differences are rational. This is relevant since the only office I could seek would be the outlander seat on the Tribal Council.

I'm generally opposed to *per capita* payments, but not so opposed that I would allow elders within the homeland to live in squalor.

Nobody with that complex of positions is going to be elected to any significant office in the Cherokee Nation unless they can obfuscate and deny.

I have always been available for service on the Cherokee Nation Supreme Court, but I disqualify myself by saying a judge cannot serve any faction. This is irrelevant anyway, because it's not within the job description of a judge to impose his ideas, let alone his dreams.

Still, I must have a Cherokee dream to write in the terms I've chosen? I do.

I want to reconstruct our land base.

I believe that if we cannot do this, the days for our culture are numbered.

The Cherokee government used to offer a history course, but that has fallen victim to factional warfare. We sponsor Cherokee language immersion in Oklahoma schools but we do not do tribal business in the Cherokee language. This is not enough policy to carry the freight of cultural preservation. We need a land base so we can live together. Culture is not a solitary enterprise.

I understand that reconstruction of a land base destroyed in 1907 is borderline crazy. So was social equality for former slaves. So was a labor union for migrant farm workers. Yes, crazy, and impossible unless it were to spread to, say, less than a third of the paper Cherokees on the current registry.

An income tax on outlanders encourages residence in the homeland and it separates the Cherokee from the hobbyist, the blood from the paper. Tribal taxes should be deductible from federal taxes on the same basis as state taxes, but we have yet to license that argument by taxing ourselves.

The next step is to sit down with a real estate "heat map" of what the Cherokee government calls its "jurisdictional area" to target the least expensive contiguous real estate. We don't need all of northeastern Oklahoma even if we could afford it.

I would suggest that the lawyers set up some shell purchasers so as not to stir up either politics or greed.

Then we just need a few tens of billions of dollars, right?

Dreaming a task as inter-generational expands what is possible.

I'd start in middle school and take my model from Cherokee history and the famous science fiction novel, *Ender's Game*. The Cherokee language used to be the language of trade. We never went to sea, but we traded with people who did. Copper smelted in Cherokee country ended up in the desert Southwest when North America was innocent of wheels and horses. Have we lost the knack?

The Cherokee Nation should own an internet service provider for profit, and divert some of that hardware to a new Heptagon on tribal lands, divided into seven trading stations for the seven clans: the Wolf Clan day trades equities, the Blue Clan swing trades equities, the Wild Potato Clan trades commodities, the Long Hair Clan trades sovereign bonds, the Deer Clan trades corporate bonds, the Bird Clan trades FOREX and the Paint Clan trades options.

Others might pick a different seven, and I jest by picking specific clans (although they are not random).   We train Cherokee kids from the homeland in fundamental and technical analysis and put the most gifted on the tribal payroll at minimum wage while they are still in high school based on tests administered at the end of the middle school finance classes not currently offered.

They come to the Heptagon every day and paper trade. If they can't follow the math, they're out. If they lose interest, they're out. If they don't improve, they're out. They are told, girls and boys, that they are training to be warriors, to fight for our lands. The standard for performance is the quality of their trades, everybody in each category having started with the same sum of paper.

All of these transactions are an agreement about price based on a disagreement about value. Fundamental analysis teaches how to determine what might be called rational value, but it's necessary to account for the *bon mot* attributed to John Maynard Keynes: "The market can stay irrational longer than you can stay solvent." So technical analysis gives us mathematical tools to anticipate market behavior, rational or not.

At some point—and the kids are not told when this happens, because they don't need any unnecessary pressure---the paper trading becomes the real thing. Most of the profits go towards the land fund, but a portion is put aside so the individuals do get to eat some of what they kill.

While they can quit when they wish, it's hard for an individual to do this sort of thing. Unless you are wealthy, day trading is on margin, and you need direct lines into the exchanges, the fastest chips, multiple screens. This takes seed money.

As in *Ender's Game*, which involved a different kind of war, kids trained to the task would smoke their elders. The biggest problem with locating such a project within tribal government would be to structure it in a manner to prevent stealing. Not by the kids, but by the adults controlling the switch from paper trades to real trades. It would probably be safer to put it out for bids with the investment banks that already have strong and secure trading platforms with integrated paper trading. And the bids are not about what the tribe pays them, but rather about what they pay the tribe in the form of reduced commissions for what would be a huge amount of business.

This is one crazy way to pursue a crazy dream using the assets of a tribal government. Those tribes that have a land base don't share this crazy dream. They may want nothing more than to control their own tribal government. Beside having to reconstruct a land base, that's a cakewalk.

Some very commercial poets wrote that "a dream is a wish your heart makes." It's appropriate that those lines are grounded in Franz Liszt at one end and Walt Disney at the other, high culture and popular culture.

A dream on the intergenerational level calls for a bit of outlandishness and for cultural moorings. MLK's dream to strike down racial segregation, the visible and legal legacy of slavery, called on an African-American tradition of resistance to slavery that was utterly invisible to persons not raised in that tradition.

It was a dream that refused to die in the face of the purposeful destruction of tribal ties, familial ties, African culture. The grand strategy of it spawned tactical sub-narratives, such as the legal crusade of Charles Hamilton Houston and Thurgood Marshall to overturn the "separate but equal" doctrine, an oppressive fantasy that had roots at least as deep as "domestic, dependent nations."

Such is the power of a dream when it can tap deep blood memories and living cultural truth. If we can't tap that power, then we shall become the historical relics the colonists wish us to be. If we can tap that power, it's past time we got started.

ABOUT THE AUTHOR

Steve Russell is a citizen of the Cherokee Nation, born and raised in the Creek Nation. He dropped out of Bristow, Oklahoma High School in the ninth grade.

After serving in the U.S. Air Force from 1964 to 1968, he graduated *magna cum laude* from the University of Texas at Austin, and went on to earn a law degree from the same school. He also received a master of judicial studies degree from the University of Nevada at Reno.

His first career was as a Texas trial court judge, first on the Austin Municipal Court and then Travis County Court at Law No. Two.

His second career was as a criminal justice professor, first at the University of Texas at San Antonio and then at Indiana University, Bloomington. He is currently Associate Professor *Emeritus* of Criminal Justice at Indiana University and retains his judicial status in Texas as well.

Twice retired, Russell lives with his wife Tracy in Georgetown, Texas. He writes regular columns on tribal affairs for *Indian Country Today Media Network* and a weekly commentary on the news in the same venue called *How Did I Miss That?*, featuring the remarks of his eccentric Republican cousin, Ray Sixkiller.

Russell is the author of *Sequoyah Rising: Problems in Post-Colonial Tribal Governance* (Carolina Academic Press 2010), *Ceremonies of Innocence: Essays from the Indian Wars* (Dog Iron Press 2012) *Ray Sixkiller's Cherokee Nation: U.S. Elections, 2012* (Dog Iron Press 2014) and *Wicked Dew* (Dog Iron Press 2012), winner of the Poetry First Book Award from the Native Writers Circle of the Americas in 2008.